My Favorite Color Is...

(Activity Coloring Book)

Illustrated by:
Iona Cordero and Stevan Mitric

Rev. date 09/01/2016
Published by Magicwonders4kidz

To order additional copies of this book visit:

www.ionacordero.com

www.amazon.com　　　　　www.barnes&noble.com

This book is dedicated
to my lovely daughter Lyza
who always wanted perfection
in her coloring
when she was little
and this was created just for you
with lots of love ...

I.C.

This book belongs to:

Name: _____

Age: _____

I am a Duck

My favorite color is...

Yellow

I am a Pig

My favorite color is...

Pink

I am a Frog

My favorite color is...

Green

I am a Cat

My favorite color is...

Orange

I am a Ant

My favorite color is...

Red

I am a Fish

My favorite color is...

Purple

I am a Octupus

My favorite color is...

Blue

I am a Cow

My favorite color is...

Brown

I am a Elephant

My favorite color is...

Gray

I am a Seal

My favorite color is...

Black

I am a Butterfly

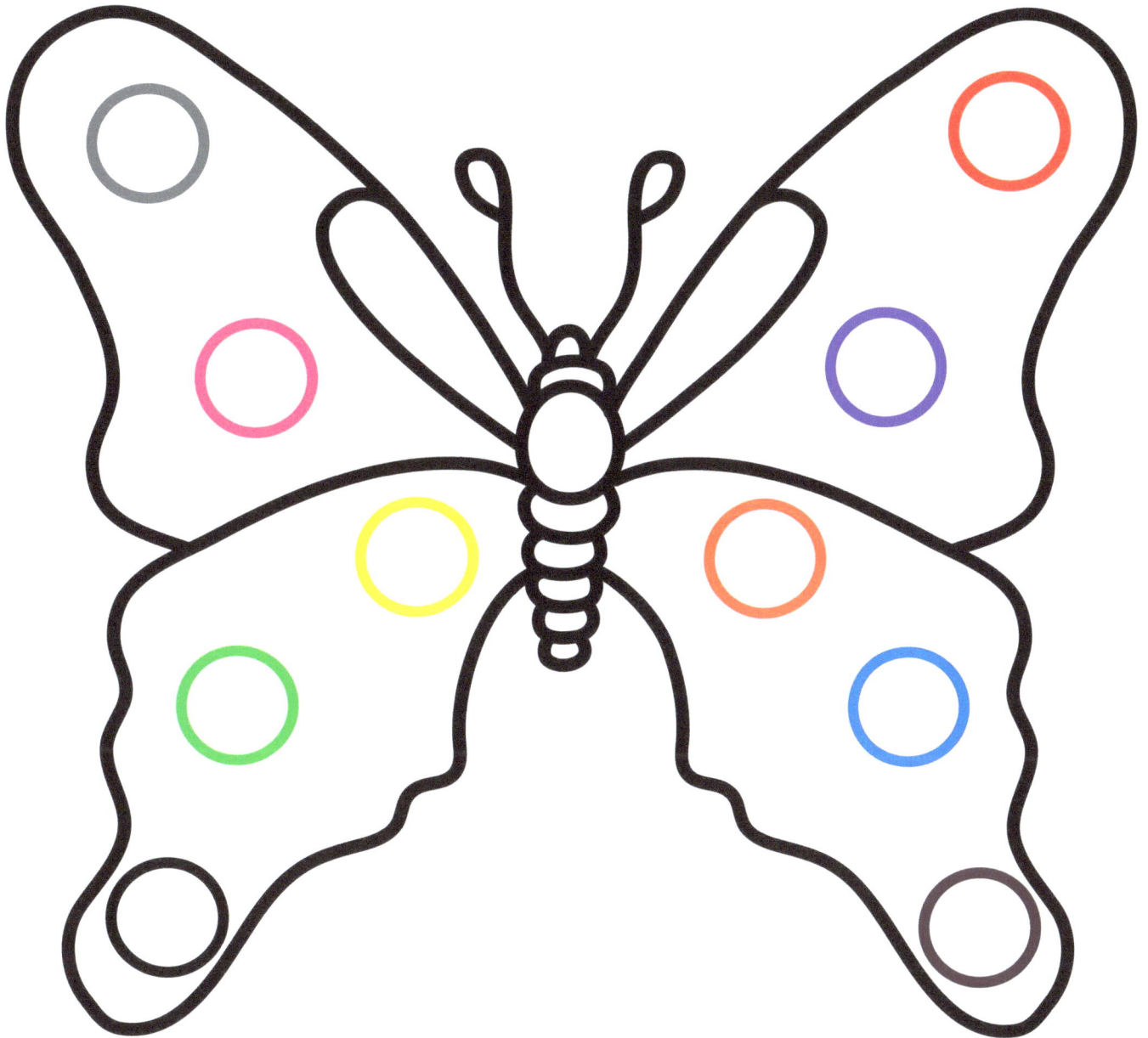

My favorite colors are...

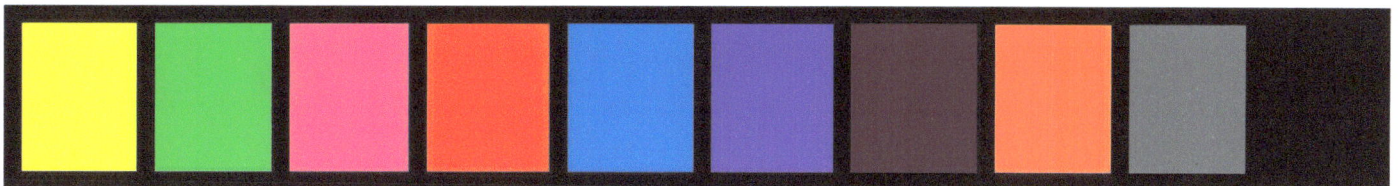

Color the Ballons

Color the Crayons

Color the Squares

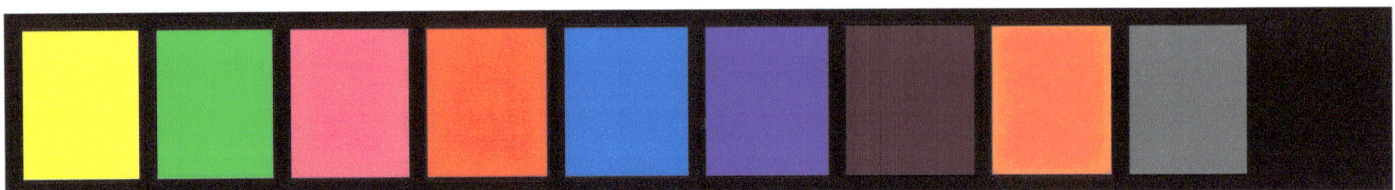

Color the Circles

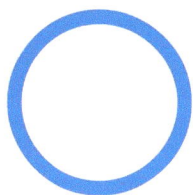

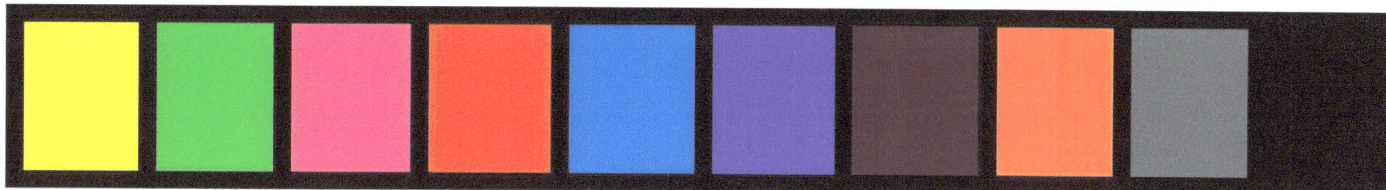

Color the Stars

Color the Shapes

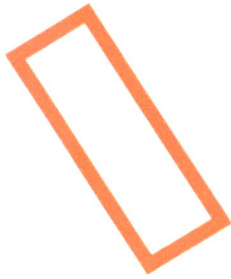

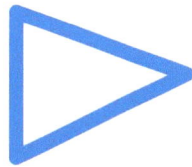

Trace Your Hands

Pick one color for each finger

Draw your favorite animal...

Use your favorite Color

What was your favorite color...

_____

What was your favorite animal...

_____